3 0214 1015 8105 7

$21.95 9/12   WLW

D0859471

ARIZONA
DIAMONDBACKS

by Rob Tricchinelli

Published by ABDO Publishing Company, 8000 West 78th Street, Edina, Minnesota 55439. Copyright © 2011 by Abdo Consulting Group, Inc. International copyrights reserved in all countries. No part of this book may be reproduced in any form without written permission from the publisher. SportsZone™ is a trademark and logo of ABDO Publishing Company.

Printed in the United States of America,
North Mankato, Minnesota
112010
012011

 THIS BOOK CONTAINS AT LEAST 10% RECYCLED MATERIALS.

Editor: Matt Tustison
Copy Editor: Nicholas Cafarelli
Interior Design and Production: Craig Hinton
Cover Design: Craig Hinton

Photo Credits: Ross D. Franklin/AP Images, cover; Matt York/AP Images, title, 11, 23, 37, 47; John Bazemore/AP Images, 4, 8, 29, 43 (top, middle), 44; Kevork Djansezian/AP Images, 7, 16, 24, 42 (middle, bottom); Mike Fiala/AP Images, 12; Scott Troyanos/AP Images, 15, 42 (top); Donald Miralle/Allsport/Getty Images, 19; David Kennedy/AP Images, 20; Marcio Jose Sanchez/AP Images, 26, 30; Khampha Bouaphanh/AP Images, 33; M. Spencer Green/AP Images, 34, 43 (bottom); Kathy Willens/AP Images, 38; J Pat Carter/AP Images, 41

Library of Congress Cataloging-in-Publication Data
Tricchinelli, Rob, 1985-
  Arizona Diamondbacks / by Rob Tricchinelli.
      p. cm.
  Includes index.
  ISBN 978-1-61714-034-1
  1. Arizona Diamondbacks (Baseball team)—History—Juvenile literature. I. Title.
  GV875.A64T75 2011
  796.357'640979173—dc22
                        2010036458

TABLE OF CONTENTS

CHAPTER 1

GLORY!

It was November 4, 2001. The Arizona Diamondbacks were in trouble. It was the bottom of the ninth inning of Game 7 of the World Series. Arizona had to score a run against the New York Yankees just to tie the game.

Mariano Rivera was pitching for New York. The previous 23 times Rivera pitched in a save situation in the postseason, the Yankees won. And he had struck out the side in the eighth inning. Arizona's Mark Grace stepped to the plate. He faced difficult odds.

The Yankees were a famously successful team. They had won 26 World Series titles, including three in a row from 1998 to 2000. The Diamondbacks were in only their fourth season as a team. They were in their first World Series.

Although it was a new team, Arizona had several veteran players. Luis Gonzalez was the team leader on offense. Grace, Steve Finley, and

Luis Gonzalez reacts after driving in the winning run in the Diamondbacks' 3–2 victory in Game 7 of the 2001 World Series.

PAIR OF ACES

Randy Johnson and Curt Schilling dominated hitters during Arizona's 2001 championship season.

Johnson, a left-hander who stood 6-foot-10, had a blazing fastball and a snapping slider. In 2001, he won his third of four consecutive Cy Young Awards as the NL's best pitcher. Johnson was 21–6 with a league-leading 2.49 earned-run average (ERA). He had a career-high 372 strikeouts, which was also the third-highest total by a pitcher in one big-league season since 1900. Schilling, a 6-foot-5 right-hander, went 22–6 in 2001 with a 2.98 ERA and 293 strikeouts.

The duo was even better in the playoffs. Schilling was 4–0 with a 1.12 ERA and 56 strikeouts in six starts. Johnson was 5–1 with a 1.52 ERA and 47 strikeouts. It was only fitting that each was named a co-Most Valuable Player (MVP) of the World Series.

Jay Bell were all longtime major league players. Starting pitchers Curt Schilling and Randy Johnson formed a one-two punch that struck fear into opposing hitters.

It had been a wild, fun ride for the team and its fans getting to the World Series. Arizona finished the regular season 92–70 and won the National League (NL) West by two games. With superb pitching and a tough veteran lineup, the Diamondbacks were prepared to succeed in the playoffs.

The Diamondbacks faced the St. Louis Cardinals in the NL Division Series (NLDS). Schilling threw a three-hit shutout at home in Game 1. He pitched again in the deciding Game 5 and had another complete game. Tony Womack's single in the bottom of the ninth gave Arizona a 2–1 win

Arizona's Curt Schilling, *left*, greets teammate Randy Johnson after Johnson pitched a shutout against Atlanta in Game 1 of the 2001 NLCS.

and a series victory. The excitement was only beginning.

Arizona's pitching starred again against the Atlanta Braves in the NL Championship Series (NLCS). Johnson hurled a three-hit shutout at home in Game 1. He struck out 11 in a 2–0 victory. Atlanta won the next game. But Schilling came through again in Game 3. He pitched another complete game and struck out 12 as Arizona won 5–1.

The Diamondbacks' offense led the way in the next game, an 11–4 victory. Thanks to another strong pitching effort by Johnson and a two-run home run by Erubiel Durazo,

The Diamondbacks' Luis Gonzalez, *left*, congratulates Tony Womack after Womack scored in Game 6 of the 2001 World Series.

the visiting Diamondbacks won 3–2 in Game 5.

The Diamondbacks made it to the World Series, baseball's biggest stage. They would face the mighty Yankees. The 2001 World Series would be considered by many baseball followers as one of the best ever.

Schilling and Johnson continued their standout pitching in the Fall Classic. Schilling went seven strong innings in Game 1. The Diamondbacks cruised to a 9–1 home victory. In Game 2, Johnson silenced the Yankees' bats with another shutout, 4–0. The series went back to New York, and the Yankees squeaked out a 2–1 win.

The Diamondbacks were ahead 3–1 in the ninth inning

of Game 4. Byung-Hyun Kim came in to close the game for Arizona. But New York's Tino Martinez crushed a two-run homer to tie it. In the 10th inning, Derek Jeter hit a solo homer off Kim to give the Yankees a victory.

Game 5 was eerily similar to Game 4 for Arizona and its fans. The Diamondbacks led 2–0 in the bottom of the ninth. But then Scott Brosius hit a two-run homer off Kim to tie the game. The Yankees won in the 12th inning. The teams headed back to Arizona.

Johnson again pitched well in Game 6. The Diamondbacks' offense also came to play, collecting 22 hits. The result was a 15–2 victory. The World Series would come down to Game 7.

The September 11, 2001, terrorist attacks that took the lives of thousands of people in New York were still fresh on the minds of New Yorkers and Americans. Major League Baseball (MLB) canceled its games for a week to help the city and the nation mourn and heal. The fact that a team from New York was in the World Series, just weeks after the attacks, gave the Fall Classic extra emotion.

So the stage was set for an epic Game 7. Schilling was

Luis Gonzalez

Diamondbacks left fielder Luis Gonzalez, known as "Gonzo," was a very popular player in Arizona. He had a season to remember in 2001. That year was Gonzalez's 12th in the major leagues, and it was his best. He batted .325 with 57 home runs and 142 runs batted in (RBIs). As a result of those numbers, he finished third in the NL MVP voting. Arizona acquired Gonzalez in a trade with the Detroit Tigers before the 1999 season. Gonzalez went on to have the best seasons of his career with the Diamondbacks. He played with Arizona through 2006. He retired from the big leagues after the 2008 season.

strong. But so was Yankees starter Roger Clemens. After seven innings, the game was tied at 1–1. In the top of the eighth, Alfonso Soriano homered off Schilling to give the Yankees a 2–1 lead. New York then brought in Rivera. He struck out the side in the bottom of the eighth.

The Yankees led 2–1 going into the bottom of the ninth. It was Grace's turn to try to make something happen. After taking a ball, Grace swung at Rivera's cutting fastball. He singled into center field.

Next, Damian Miller stepped up to the plate. He tried to bunt. Diamondbacks manager Bob Brenly wanted to advance the runner to second base. Miller's bunt bounced right back to Rivera. But Rivera threw off target to second base. Everyone was safe. There were two on with no outs.

Bell came up and bunted. The ball again bounced to Rivera. Rivera made the throw to third for the first out of the ninth. Womack, the leadoff man, was up next. He ripped a 2–2 fastball down the right-field line for a double. Pinch-runner Midre Cummings raced home. The game was tied.

Craig Counsell came to bat. Rivera's fastball cut too far inside and hit him. The bases were loaded. Gonzalez stepped into the batter's box.

Yankees manager Joe Torre brought his fielders in to keep the runner on third from scoring on a softly hit ball. The Yankees' infielders played along the front of the infield dirt.

After a strike, Gonzalez swung. He connected. The ball blooped over the head of Jeter, the Yankees' shortstop. Bell raced home, and the

Diamondbacks players, including Steve Finley, *center*, celebrate after winning the 2001 World Series. Arizona was in just its fourth season.

Diamondbacks swarmed the field. They had beaten Rivera and the tradition-rich Yankees. They were world champions.

The Diamondbacks won the championship in just their fourth season. No other team has gone from its founding to the World Series title so fast.

Arizona began playing in 1998. The Diamondbacks and the Tampa Bay Rays, who also started playing in 1998, have the shortest histories of any teams in the major leagues. Still, the Diamondbacks have taken their fans on a roller coaster of ups and downs. The biggest thrill has been the 2001 World Series title.

CHAPTER 2

THE BEGINNINGS

Jerry Colangelo had dreamed of landing a big-league baseball team in Arizona. In the early 1990s, Colangelo started working toward making that dream a reality. He already owned the Phoenix Suns of the National Basketball Association. He put together a group of businessmen who were eager to see a baseball team play in the state.

In 1995, the efforts of Colangelo and his business partners paid off. MLB announced on March 9 of that year that Colangelo's group had been awarded a big-league team.

The Tampa Bay, Florida, area was also granted a team. Both would begin playing in 1998.

MLB especially liked the part of Colangelo's bid that said his team would play in a new stadium with a retractable roof. The team would be able to open and close the roof as needed.

Jerry Colangelo, shown in 1998, headed a group of businessmen who brought a new big-league baseball team to Arizona.

BUCK SHOWALTER

Buck Showalter, the Diamondbacks' first manager, played in the New York Yankees' farm system as a first baseman but never made it to the majors. He then got into coaching and managing with the Yankees' minor league teams. In 1990, Showalter was promoted to New York's big-league staff. In 1992, he became manager. Three years later, he led the Yankees to the playoffs. He and owner George Steinbrenner did not see eye to eye, however, and Showalter left. The Yankees won the World Series the next year.

The Diamondbacks hired Showalter as their manager in November 1995. He led the team to back-to-back winning campaigns in 1999 and 2000. But expectations became high very quickly in Arizona, and Showalter was let go. For the second time, his old team won the World Series the year after he left. Showalter later managed the Texas Rangers and the Baltimore Orioles.

On especially hot days in Arizona, the roof could be closed to keep fans more comfortable in an air-conditioned environment. The ballpark would be located in downtown Phoenix.

The Arizona team was named the Diamondbacks. That choice was the winning entry in a contest in the *Arizona Republic* newspaper in 1995. The Western diamondback is a rattlesnake native to the southwest region of the United States. The new team's colors would be turquoise, copper, black, and purple.

Buck Showalter was hired as Arizona's first manager. He had managed the New York Yankees from 1992 to 1995 and led them to one playoff appearance. The hire came in November 1995. This was more than two years before the Diamondbacks would play a game. Arizona wanted

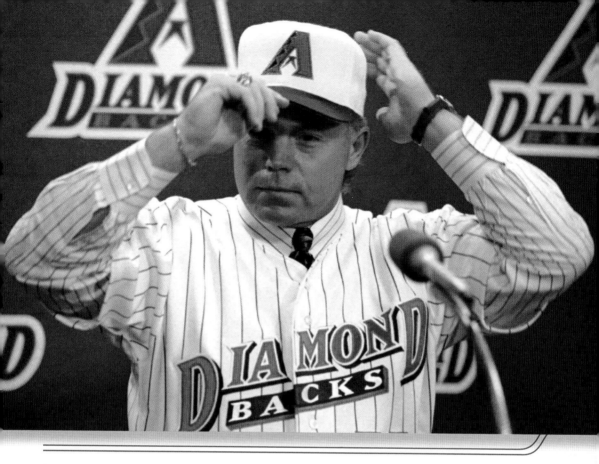

Buck Showalter puts on an Arizona cap in November 1995. The team had officially named him as the Diamondbacks' first manager.

Showalter's help in deciding which players to select for the new team.

Arizona participated in MLB's amateur draft for the first time on June 4, 1996. With their first draft selection, the Diamondbacks chose left-handed pitcher Nick Bierbrodt with the 30th pick overall.

In addition to the annual amateur draft, Arizona added players in a special expansion draft on November 18, 1997. That day, the Diamondbacks and Tampa Bay's team, the Devil Rays, selected players made available by the existing MLB teams. Arizona's first two selections in the draft were pitchers

Randy Johnson pitches in 1999. Johnson signed with the Diamondbacks before that season and helped the team win the NL West.

Brian Anderson and Jeff Suppan. The Diamondbacks also added some players through free agency (such as shortstop Jay Bell) and trades (such as third baseman Matt Williams) before their first season.

The Diamondbacks were ready to play ball. Arizona was placed in the NL West Division with Colorado, the Los Angeles Dodgers, San Diego, and San Francisco.

Like most expansion teams, Arizona struggled at first. The team finished 1998 with a 65–97 record. At the All-Star break, the Diamondbacks were 30–58. After the break, however, Arizona went a promising 35–39. This excited the many fans who turned out to see them at the new stadium, Bank One Ballpark.

Arizona turned from a losing team to a winning team quickly. The crown jewel of the next off-season was ace pitcher Randy Johnson. He signed a four-year contract with the Diamondbacks worth $52 million. The contract had an option for a fifth year. Johnson finished the 1998 season with the Houston Astros after playing for the Seattle Mariners for many seasons. He passed up offers from teams with winning records in 1998, including Houston, to join Arizona. He had just built a large house near Phoenix.

The Diamondbacks also signed center fielder Steve Finley and relief pitcher Byung-Hyun Kim as free agents and acquired left fielder Luis Gonzalez from the Detroit Tigers.

The pieces of a successful team were coming together. Arizona started the season just 14–14 but then began to excel. The Diamondbacks finished 100–62 and ran away with the NL West. Finley, Bell, and Williams all topped 30 home runs. Those three and Gonzalez all had more than 100 RBIs. Speedy Tony Womack stole an NL-best 72 bases. He had been acquired from the Pittsburgh Pirates before the season.

The biggest story in 1999 for the Diamondbacks, however, was Johnson. The tall, intimidating left-hander went 17–9 with a 2.48 ERA. His 364 strikeouts led the NL by more than 140. Johnson earned his second Cy Young Award. It was his first in the NL.

Arizona and its fans were pumped up for the team's first postseason appearance. The Diamondbacks would face the

New York Mets in the first round, the NLDS. The Mets had earned the NL's wild-card spot.

In Game 1 of the NLDS, the Diamondbacks and the Mets were tied at 4–4 in the ninth inning at Bank One Ballpark. Johnson was still pitching for Arizona. But he came out of the game after loading the bases with one out. Bobby Chouinard came in to pitch for the Diamondbacks. Chouinard got Rickey Henderson to ground out. But with two outs, Edgardo Alfonzo belted a grand slam. The Mets prevailed 8–4.

Arizona won 7–1 in Game 2. But New York came back strong in Game 3. The Mets pulled away for a 9–2 victory.

The Diamondbacks needed a win in Game 4. Arizona came up in the eighth inning down 2–1. A two-out double by Bell gave the Diamondbacks a 3–2 lead. But the Mets tied the score in the bottom of the inning. After a scoreless ninth, Arizona went down in order in the top of the 10th. With one out in the bottom of the inning, Todd Pratt came up against Diamondbacks closer Matt Mantei. Pratt was not a slugger. But he became a hero with a game-winning home run. The Shea Stadium crowd went wild as the Mets won the series in an upset.

Arizona was disappointed in its playoff performance. But the team had reason to be proud, and the future appeared to be bright. The Diamondbacks had quickly built a talented group of players.

In 2000, the Diamondbacks added a second star pitcher. They traded four players—pitchers Omar Daal, Nelson Figueroa, and Vicente Padilla and first baseman/outfielder Travis Lee—to the Philadelphia

Luis Gonzalez homers during Game 1 of the 1999 NLDS. The Diamondbacks, in their first playoff series, lost three games to one to the Mets.

Phillies for veteran right-hander Curt Schilling on July 26. The Diamondbacks slumped toward the end of the 2000 season, however. They finished 85–77 for third place in the NL West.

After the 2000 season, the Diamondbacks fired Showalter as manager. This demonstrated how much Colangelo wanted to win. Former big-league catcher Bob Brenly was hired to replace Showalter. Brenly had been a coach with the San Francisco Giants.

Despite the managerial change, the pieces were there for the Diamondbacks to continue contending. In 2001, Arizona would make that apparent with its glorious run to the World Series title.

CHAPTER 3

AFTER THE CHAMPIONSHIP

T he disappointment of 1999 and 2000 turned into the excitement of 2001 for the Diamondbacks. Led by the dominant one-two combination of starting pitchers Curt Schilling and Randy Johnson, Arizona won a thrilling World Series over the New York Yankees.

The Diamondbacks had only been playing in the big leagues for four years, and they were already champions. Some baseball fans have to wait decades before seeing their teams win a title. The Diamondbacks were the first team to win a World Series in such a short time. The Florida Marlins had previously been the quickest. The Marlins won

Big Parade

More than 300,000 people swarmed to Bank One Ballpark and the surrounding area on November 7, 2001, to celebrate the Diamondbacks' World Series title. The parade celebrated the first championship by a major professional sports team in Arizona.

Diamondbacks catcher Rod Barajas sits in the dugout after the St. Louis Cardinals swept Arizona in three games in the 2002 NLDS.

STEVE FINLEY

Center fielder Steve Finley played for eight major league teams over his 19-year career. Finley, who threw and hit left-handed, was a Diamondback from 1999 to 2004. He won five Gold Glove Awards in his career for his fielding abilities, and he showed great speed early in his playing days. Finley stole more than 30 bases in three seasons, and he was in his league's top 10 in triples nine times. He twice led his league in triples.

Finley played in college at Southern Illinois. The Baltimore Orioles drafted him in 1987, and he broke into the majors with that team in 1989.

Finley's stolen-base totals dipped over time, but his home-run numbers increased. Like teammate Luis Gonzalez, Finley was a wiry power hitter. He hit 30 or more home runs in a season four times. Finley retired after playing with the Colorado Rockies in 2007.

the 1997 World Series in their fifth year.

After the 2001 season, a few minor players came and went for the Diamondbacks. But the core of tough, gritty veterans remained. Arizona fans had high expectations for the team. A repeat championship seemed like a definite possibility. Schilling and Johnson dominated hitters again in 2002. Luis Gonzalez and Steve Finley powered the lineup. Johnson won another Cy Young Award, his fourth in a row. He led the league in ERA (2.32), wins (24), and strikeouts (334).

The Diamondbacks finished 98–64 in 2002 and won the NL West for the third time in four seasons. They met the St. Louis Cardinals in the NLDS for a second consecutive year. Things got off to a rocky start in the playoffs for

Center fielder Steve Finley follows the ball before making a catch in 2002. Finley, a standout defensive player, was a Diamondback from 1999 to 2004.

Arizona, however, and never improved. In the first game of the NLDS, St. Louis hit Johnson hard. The visiting Cardinals scored six runs in six innings off the left-hander and blew out the Diamondbacks 12–2.

In Game 2, Schilling tried to change the series' direction. He pitched well, giving up only one run in seven innings. But Arizona only scored one run. With the game tied in the ninth, St. Louis' Edgar Renteria singled and advanced to second base on a bunt. Then, Miguel Cairo singled to center field and Renteria scored.

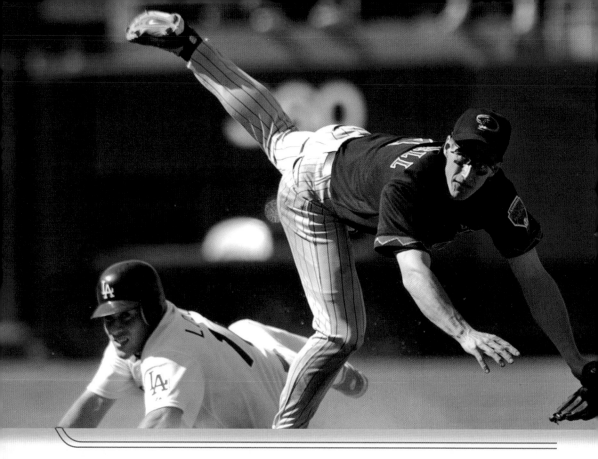

The Diamondbacks' Craig Counsell avoids the Dodgers' Paul Lo Duca at second base and keeps his balance after throwing to first in 2003. Arizona finished 84–78 that year and did not qualify for the postseason.

The Diamondbacks went down 1–2–3 in the ninth and lost.

The series went to St. Louis, and the Cardinals swept the Diamondbacks with a 6–3 victory. After all the hope for a repeat, Arizona was eliminated without winning a single postseason game.

Johnson was 39 going into the 2003 season. He and some of the other veterans were starting to show their age. Finley was 38, Schilling was 36, and Gonzalez was 35. The four of them were the Diamondbacks' biggest stars going back to the World Series season. They had carried Arizona to the playoffs again in 2002. But their run of success would not last.

In 2003, Johnson was bothered by injuries, especially to his right knee. He only made 18 starts and was 6–8 with a 4.26 ERA. The Diamondbacks struggled on offense, too. Schilling had a 2.95 ERA but only an 8–9 record. He did not get very much run support. Neither did rookie Brandon Webb. Webb's final record was just 10–9 despite having a 2.84 ERA. Although Gonzalez and Finley were steady, the rest of the offense did not have much pop.

Arizona finished 84–78 and missed the playoffs by seven games. A lot of players' contracts were ending. The team was losing money. The World Series title-winning season, which happened just two years before, seemed like a distant memory. Changes were

Tony Womack

He is best known for his clutch double off Yankees closer Mariano Rivera in Game 7 of the 2001 World Series. But there was more to Tony Womack than just that one play. Womack had a productive big-league career as an outfielder/ infielder. His main asset was his speed. He was a leadoff batter for the Diamondbacks. He led the NL in stolen bases three straight years, from 1997 to 1999. The last of those seasons came with the Diamondbacks. He had a career-high 72 steals that year. He then swiped at least 28 bases each season from 2000 to 2002. In 2000, he led the NL with 14 triples. In July 2003, the Diamondbacks traded Womack to the Colorado Rockies. Womack retired in 2006 with 363 steals in 13 big-league seasons.

coming. Unfortunately for the Diamondbacks, they were not going to work out well.

CHAPTER 4

THE TUMBLE

Diamondbacks owner Jerry Colangelo spent a lot of money to bring veteran players to his team during the early part of its history. It worked very well for a while. Arizona won the World Series in just its fourth season in 2001.

But having a roster with several aging players was not a recipe for long-term success. To be good in the long haul, the Diamondbacks knew they needed a core of young talent to build around.

As a result, a lot of players moved around after the Diamondbacks finished the 2003 season a disappointing 84–78.

Arizona traded star pitcher Curt Schilling to the Boston Red Sox for pitchers Jorge De La Rosa, Casey Fossum, and Brandon Lyon and outfielder Michael Goss. First baseman Mark Grace retired. Starting pitcher Miguel Batista signed with the Toronto Blue Jays.

A month after Schilling was dealt, Arizona sent six players,

Diamondbacks pitcher Casey Fossum reacts after allowing a home run to the Giants' Barry Bonds in 2004. Arizona finished the season a major league-worst 51–111.

including infielder Craig Counsell, to the Milwaukee Brewers in exchange for first baseman Richie Sexson.

The trades turned out terribly for the Diamondbacks. Sexson badly injured his left shoulder and only played in 23 games in 2004. He did have nine home runs and 23 RBIs in those games. But he hit just .233. Fossum also fared poorly.

Perfection

Randy Johnson was 40 years old when he began the 2004 season. But he still had a dominant season, and he was still a smart pitcher who could fool hitters. On May 18 against the host Atlanta Braves, Johnson threw the 17th perfect game in major league history. He retired all 27 batters he faced in the Diamondbacks' 2–0 victory. He struck out 13 Braves and became the oldest pitcher in big-league history to throw a perfect game. It was also the second no-hitter of Johnson's career. The first came back in 1990, when he was with the Seattle Mariners.

He was a left-hander who had spent some time in the majors with the Red Sox. He was seen as a key player in the Schilling trade. Fossum went 4–15 with a 6.65 ERA for Arizona in 2004. Meanwhile, the departed Schilling starred for Boston that season as it won the World Series for the first time since 1918.

Sexson and Fossum were not the only problems. The Diamondbacks' lineup was weak. Only one full-time player, infielder Shea Hillenbrand, had a batting average higher than .300. Steve Finley's 23 home runs were a team high. But he only drove in 48 runs. Hillenbrand led the team with 80 RBIs. Finley was traded in the middle of the season to the Los Angeles Dodgers in a deal that brought three prospects.

There were very few bright spots for the Diamondbacks in

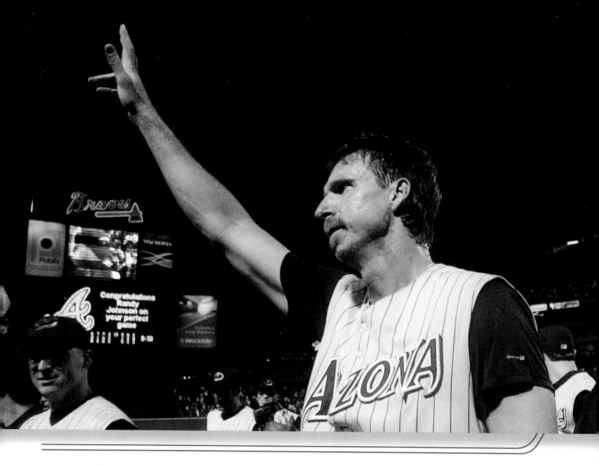

Randy Johnson waves to the crowd in Atlanta after he pitched a perfect game in the Diamondbacks' 2–0 win over the Braves on May 18, 2004.

2004. Randy Johnson was one, though. He went 16–14 with a 2.60 ERA and an NL-leading 290 strikeouts. He finished second in the Cy Young Award race to the Houston Astros' Roger Clemens.

All the changes that Arizona made before and during the 2004 season added up to a major league-worst 51–111 record. The mark was one of the 10 worst in the previous 100 years of big-league baseball. Manager Bob Brenly was fired during the season. Al Pedrique, who was managing the Diamondbacks' Triple-A affiliate in Tucson, took over as Arizona's manager on a temporary basis.

The Diamondbacks' Troy Glaus is congratulated after he homered in 2005. The slugger played well in his one season with Arizona, belting 37 homers.

After 2004, Sexson and Fossum never played for the Diamondbacks again. Sexson left as a free agent. He signed with the Seattle Mariners. Fossum was traded to the Tampa Bay Devil Rays for outfielder Jose Cruz.

Colangelo's business partners were unhappy with how far the team had fallen in three short years. They teamed up and made him resign as managing general partner. Colangelo also sold the part of the team he owned. His time in charge of the Diamondbacks was like a roller coaster. He got off at the low point.

Arizona hired Bob Melvin as its manager in November

2004. Melvin had been Seattle's manager in 2003 and 2004, before the team decided to not renew his contract. Melvin was a former major league catcher who served as a backup to Brenly with the San Francisco Giants.

The Diamondbacks made several other changes that off-season. The biggest was that the team traded its ace pitcher, Johnson, to the New York Yankees in January 2005 for right-hander Javier Vazquez and two other players. Arizona's new management was trying to rebuild the team. But it did not hesitate to spend freely, just as Colangelo had in the past. The Diamondbacks signed third baseman Troy Glaus to a long-term contract worth about $10 million each year. Arizona also signed right-handed pitcher Russ Ortiz to a contract worth more than $7 million per year.

The moves had mixed results in 2005. Vazquez struggled. He went 11–15 with a 4.42 ERA. Ortiz pitched poorly. He had a 5–11 record and 6.89 ERA in 22 starts. Glaus, however, had 37 homers and 97 RBIs. The team also got boosts from first baseman Tony Clark (30 homers) and pitcher Brandon Webb (14–12 with a 3.54 ERA). Arizona improved its record significantly from the year before. The team finished 77–85. The Diamondbacks ended up in second place in a weak NL West, five games behind the San Diego Padres.

After the season, the Diamondbacks were back to wheeling and dealing. They traded Vazquez to the Chicago White Sox for pitchers Orlando Hernandez and Luis Vizcaino and prospect Chris Young, an outfielder. Arizona then dealt Glaus and pitching prospect

BRANDON WEBB

After the Diamondbacks traded star pitchers Curt Schilling and Randy Johnson, right-hander Brandon Webb stepped up to become Arizona's ace. Webb won the NL Cy Young Award in 2006. He went 16–8 with a 3.10 ERA and 178 strikeouts.

Webb made his Diamondbacks debut in 2003, when he went 10–9 with a 2.84 ERA and finished third in the NL Rookie of the Year voting. He slumped to a 7–16 record the next season, even though his ERA was only 3.59. He improved to 14–12 with a 3.54 ERA in 2005, then emerged with the Cy Young season in 2006.

Webb continued to excel, going 18–10 with a 3.01 ERA in 2007 and 22–7 with a 3.30 ERA in 2008. He finished second in the Cy Young voting both seasons. A shoulder injury that required surgery sidelined Webb in 2009 and 2010.

Sergio Santos to Toronto for Batista—the former Diamondback—and second baseman Orlando Hudson.

Meanwhile, the Diamondbacks were seeing signs of improvement. Webb was emerging as a standout. Young, promising players were coming up though the minor leagues. In 2006, many of them received big-league playing time. These players included infielders Conor Jackson and Stephen Drew, outfielders Young and Carlos Quentin, and catcher Chris Snyder.

Arizona went 76–86 in 2006. The record was just one game worse than the team's mark in 2005. But this time the Diamondbacks finished fourth in the NL West. Still, there were many encouraging signs. The biggest development was that Webb had become one of

Arizona's Brandon Webb prepares to let go of a pitch in 2006. The right-hander emerged with a big season and won the NL Cy Young Award.

baseball's top pitchers. He finished 16–8 with a 3.10 ERA to win the NL Cy Young Award. Meanwhile, Bank One Ballpark's name had changed to Chase Field.

After the season, popular left fielder Luis Gonzalez departed to sign with the Los Angeles Dodgers. The Diamondbacks were going with a youth movement. They declined a $10 million option to bring Gonzalez back for the next season. Gonzalez left as the most successful hitter in Diamondbacks history. But as the legendary player went elsewhere, Arizona's youngsters would give the team's fans reason to be excited.

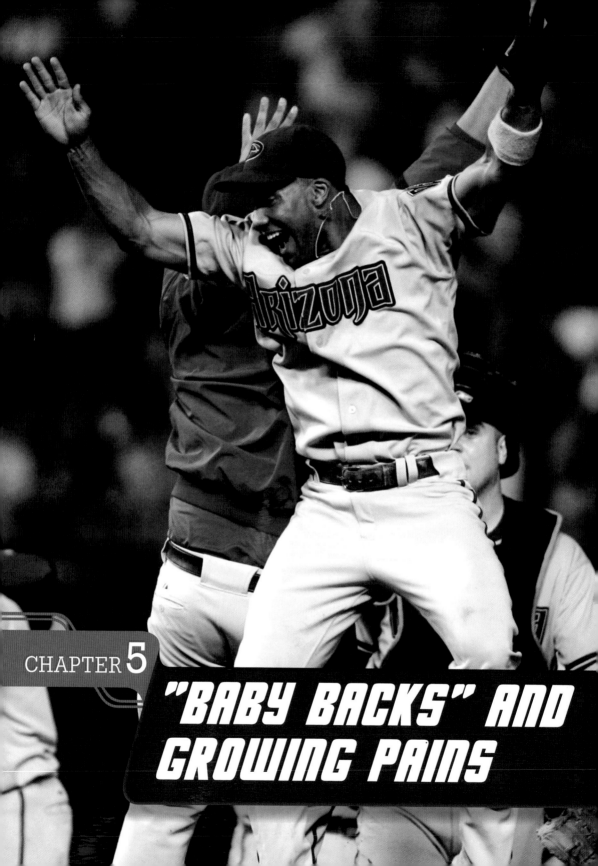

CHAPTER 5

"BABY BACKS" AND GROWING PAINS

By the time the 2007 season arrived, youth had taken over for Arizona. Only one regular starter was older than 30. The Diamondbacks began to be called the "Baby Backs."

Arizona had a young, energetic lineup and four consistent starting pitchers. Hard-throwing Jose Valverde took over as closer. Before the season, the team traded with the New York Yankees to bring back star pitcher Randy Johnson, giving up four players.

The Baby Backs finished 90–72 in 2007 and captured the NL West title by just beating out the second-place Colorado Rockies. Arizona was headed back to the postseason for the first time since 2002. A back injury sidelined Johnson for much of the season. But other players made up for his absence. Brandon Webb was the Cy Young runner-up after going 18–10. Center fielder Chris Young

Rookie Chris Young celebrates after the Diamondbacks completed a sweep of the Cubs in the 2007 NLDS with a 5–1 victory in Game 3.

JUSTIN UPTON

Right fielder Justin Upton's big-league debut with Arizona in 2007 was highly anticipated. The Diamondbacks had selected the Virginia native with the top overall pick in the 2005 amateur draft. He rose through the team's minor league system and made his major league debut in August 2007. Upton was a little more than three weeks away from turning 20 years old.

Upton finished the 2007 regular season with a .221 batting average and two home runs in 140 at-bats. He then excelled in the 2007 postseason, batting .357.

An injury sidelined Upton for part of the 2008 season, but he still finished with 15 homers in 108 games. In 2009, he had 26 homers and 86 RBIs to go along with 20 stolen bases as he earned his first All-Star spot. He compiled similar numbers in 2010, confirming that he was one of baseball's best young talents.

belted 32 home runs in his first full big-league season. Rookie third baseman Mark Reynolds added 17 homers.

The Diamondbacks met the Chicago Cubs in the NLDS. Webb allowed just four hits and one run in seven innings as host Arizona won 3–1 in Game 1. Reynolds and fellow youngster Stephen Drew homered for the Diamondbacks. A three-run homer by Young lifted Arizona to an 8–4 victory in Game 2. The Diamondbacks completed a sweep with a 5–1 road win in Game 3. Livan Hernandez pitched six strong innings for Arizona.

In the next round, the NLCS, the Diamondbacks faced a division rival, the wild-card Rockies. The Rockies were also young and energetic. They had swept the Philadelphia Phillies in the NLDS.

Justin Upton prepares to bat in Game 1 of the 2007 NLCS against Colorado. The right fielder, one of Arizona's "Baby Backs," was just 20 years old at the time. Unfortunately for the Diamondbacks, they were swept by the Rockies.

In Game 1 of the NLCS, visiting Colorado was leading 5–1 in the seventh inning when Arizona tried to rally. On a ground ball, Diamondbacks rookie Justin Upton slid hard into second base. He was trying to break up a potential double play. The umpire ruled that Upton interfered with the second baseman and awarded Colorado two outs. Arizona fans, angered, threw bottles and garbage onto the field. After a delay, the game resumed and the Rockies won 5–1.

In Game 2, the Diamondbacks lost 3–2 after Valverde

Dan Haren, hurling a pitch in 2008, helped Arizona contend for the NL West crown that year. The team, however, faded late in the season.

gave up a bases-loaded walk in the 11th inning. A three-run homer by Yorvit Torrealba lifted Colorado to a 4–1 home victory in Game 3. The Rockies then looked to complete a sweep in Game 4. The Diamondbacks trailed 6–1 going into the eighth inning. Chris Snyder hit a three-run homer for Arizona that inning. But the comeback ended there. Colorado prevailed 6–4 to win the series four games to none. The Boston Red Sox would sweep the Rockies in the World Series.

The season did not end the way that Arizona would have liked. But with a group of talented young players leading the way, the Diamondbacks' future seemed very promising.

Before the 2008 season, Arizona let go of a handful of prospects to acquire pitcher Dan Haren from the Oakland Athletics. For most of the 2008 season, things were looking just fine for Arizona. The Diamondbacks held the NL West lead for much of the season. Haren and Webb pitched very well. Johnson, who had returned from his back injury, was a solid third starter at the age of 44. The team's young lineup was also producing.

After a 4–3 home win over the St. Louis Cardinals on September 3, the Diamondbacks led the NL West by 1 1/2 games. Arizona, however, then went on a six-game losing streak. The Diamondbacks finished 82–80 and in second place, two games behind the Los Angeles Dodgers.

From Purple to Red

The Diamondbacks spent their early years with the same cool-colored uniforms featuring turquoise, copper, black, and purple. But for the 2007 season, the team got a new look, like a snake after shedding its skin. The Diamondbacks switched to a warmer color scheme. The uniforms became Sedona Red, black, and sand, better reflecting the hot, dry environment in the Arizona desert. The team also changed the writing on the front of its jerseys, putting "Arizona" on the gray road uniforms and "D-backs" on the home white uniforms.

The Diamondbacks were upset about their poor finish in 2008. But they still had reasons to be optimistic. Their young players had continued to play well. The starting pitching, led by Webb (22–7) and Haren (16–8), also was a strength.

But things would not work out well for Arizona in 2009. First, Johnson signed with his hometown San Francisco Giants. He would go 8–6 in

Mark Reynolds

Diamondbacks third baseman Mark Reynolds arrived in the major leagues in 2007. The 6-foot-2, 220-pound slugger showed that he could hit home runs, but also that he would strike out often. Reynolds finished his first season with 17 homers in 111 games. He also struck out 129 times. That pattern would repeat itself, as he hit 28, 44, and 32 homers, respectively, in 2008, 2009, and 2010 but also led the majors with 204, 223, and 211 strikeouts. The 223 strikeouts broke the major league single-season record that Reynolds had set the previous year.

his final big-league season and finish with a career record of 303–166.

Johnson's departure hurt the Diamondbacks. But even more troublesome was Webb's right shoulder injury that occurred on Opening Day against visiting Colorado. Webb had surgery on the shoulder in August and missed the rest of the 2009 season. He also would miss the 2010 season because of the injury.

In addition to losing Webb and Johnson, Arizona's struggles in 2009 could be attributed to the drop in production from some of the team's young players. Reynolds (44 homers, 102 RBIs) and Upton (.300 batting average, 26 homers) fared the best of those players. But it was not enough to carry the team. Haren, at 14–10, was the team's only starting pitcher with a winning record. The Diamondbacks finished 70–92 and in last place in the NL West. Manager Bob Melvin was fired about a month into the season. A. J. Hinch, the Diamondbacks' manager of minor league operations, replaced Melvin.

The 2010 season did not go any better for Arizona. With Webb still out, the team's lack of quality pitching was again a problem. With the

Mark Reynolds watches one of the 44 home runs he smashed in 2009. Reynolds became known for hitting homers but also striking out often.

Diamondbacks out of contention in July, they traded Haren to the Los Angeles Angels for left-handed pitcher Joe Saunders and three prospects. Arizona finished in last place for a second consecutive season. Hinch was fired in early July after the team started 31–48. Bench coach Kirk Gibson, a former star outfielder in the big leagues, replaced Hinch on an interim basis.

The Baby Backs were no longer babies. If the Diamondbacks were to return to the playoffs, those players would need to live up to the promise they had shown in 2007 and 2008.

| 1995 | On March 9, a group of investors led by Jerry Colangelo is awarded an MLB franchise for Phoenix, Arizona. The group decides to name the team the Arizona Diamondbacks. |

| 1995 | Former New York Yankees manager Buck Showalter is hired as the Diamondbacks' first manager on November 15. The team was still more than two years away from playing a game. |

| 1998 | After finishing their first season 65–97, the Diamondbacks sign ace pitcher Randy Johnson to a four-year, $52 million free-agent contract on November 30. On December 28, Arizona acquires left fielder Luis Gonzalez from the Detroit Tigers for Karim Garcia, an outfielder. |

| 1999 | On September 24, Johnson pitches the Diamondbacks to an 11–3 victory over the host San Francisco Giants, clinching the NL West Division title. Arizona finishes the season 100–62. |

| 1999 | Todd Pratt's home run in the bottom of the 10th inning lifts the Mets to a 4–3 victory over the Diamondbacks in Game 4 of the NLDS on October 9, securing the series win for New York. |

| 2000 | The Diamondbacks acquire pitcher Curt Schilling from the Philadelphia Phillies for four players. |

| 2000 | On October 2, the Diamondbacks fire Showalter as manager after the team finished in third place in the NL West at 85–77. Bob Brenly would replace him. |

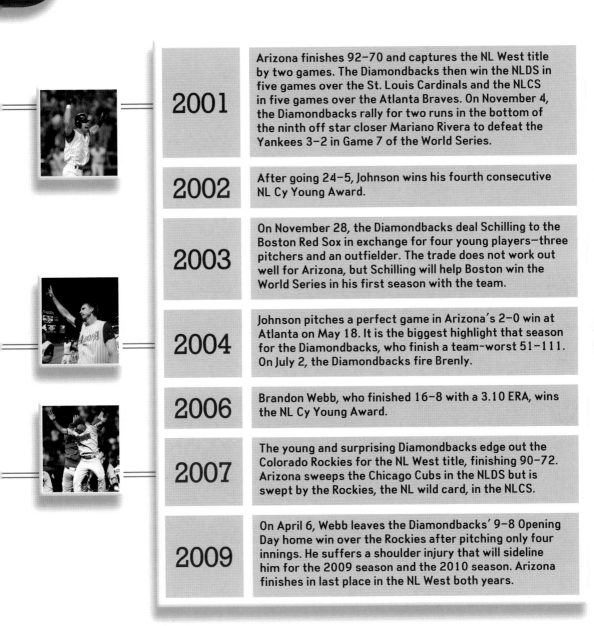

2001
Arizona finishes 92–70 and captures the NL West title by two games. The Diamondbacks then win the NLDS in five games over the St. Louis Cardinals and the NLCS in five games over the Atlanta Braves. On November 4, the Diamondbacks rally for two runs in the bottom of the ninth off star closer Mariano Rivera to defeat the Yankees 3–2 in Game 7 of the World Series.

2002
After going 24–5, Johnson wins his fourth consecutive NL Cy Young Award.

2003
On November 28, the Diamondbacks deal Schilling to the Boston Red Sox in exchange for four young players—three pitchers and an outfielder. The trade does not work out well for Arizona, but Schilling will help Boston win the World Series in his first season with the team.

2004
Johnson pitches a perfect game in Arizona's 2–0 win at Atlanta on May 18. It is the biggest highlight that season for the Diamondbacks, who finish a team-worst 51–111. On July 2, the Diamondbacks fire Brenly.

2006
Brandon Webb, who finished 16–8 with a 3.10 ERA, wins the NL Cy Young Award.

2007
The young and surprising Diamondbacks edge out the Colorado Rockies for the NL West title, finishing 90–72. Arizona sweeps the Chicago Cubs in the NLDS but is swept by the Rockies, the NL wild card, in the NLCS.

2009
On April 6, Webb leaves the Diamondbacks' 9–8 Opening Day home win over the Rockies after pitching only four innings. He suffers a shoulder injury that will sideline him for the 2009 season and the 2010 season. Arizona finishes in last place in the NL West both years.

QUICK STATS

FRANCHISE HISTORY

1998–

WORLD SERIES
(wins in bold)
2001

NL CHAMPIONSHIP SERIES

2001, 2007

DIVISION CHAMPIONSHIPS

1999, 2001, 2002, 2007

WILD-CARD BERTHS

None

KEY PLAYERS
(position[s]; seasons with team)

Jay Bell (IF; 1998–2002)
Craig Counsell (IF; 2000–03,
    2005–06)
Steve Finley (CF; 1999–2004)
Luis Gonzalez (LF; 1999–2006)
Randy Johnson (SP; 1999–2004,
    2007–08)
Mark Reynolds (3B; 2007–)
Curt Schilling (SP; 2000–03)
Justin Upton (RF; 2007–)
Brandon Webb (SP; 2003–)
Matt Williams (3B; 1998–2003)
Tony Womack (OF/IF; 1999–2003)
Chris Young (CF; 2006–)

KEY MANAGERS

Bob Brenly (2001–04):
    303–262; 11–9 (postseason)
Bob Melvin (2004–09):
    337–340; 3–4 (postseason)
Buck Showalter (1998–2000):
    250–236; 1–3 (postseason)

HOME FIELDS

Chase Field (1998–)
    Known as Bank One Ballpark
    (1998–2005)

* All statistics through 2010 season

QUOTES AND ANECDOTES

Randy Johnson was known over his long career as an overpowering pitcher. The 6-foot-10 Johnson was very intimidating and had one of baseball's best fastballs. One unlucky bird found out the hard way. In a Diamondbacks spring-training game against the San Francisco Giants on March 24, 2001, in Tucson, Arizona, a bird flew across the field and was struck by the lanky left-hander's fastball in the seventh inning. The bird's feathers flew all over when it was hit. Unfortunately, the bird did not survive. "I'm sitting there waiting for [the ball], and I'm expecting to catch the thing and all you see is an explosion," Arizona catcher Rod Barajas said. The home-plate umpire called it a "no pitch." Johnson felt badly about the accident.

In addition to having a retractable roof, one of the most noteworthy features of the Diamondbacks' home stadium, Chase Field, is that it there is a swimming pool just beyond the fence in right-center field. The pool is rented to fans as a suite, and it can hold about 40 people. Home-run balls occasionally land in the water.

After the Diamondbacks won the World Series in 2001, Randy Johnson and Curt Schilling were named Sportsmen of the Year by *Sports Illustrated* magazine. The Los Angeles Dodgers' Orel Hershiser, in 1988, had been the last pitcher to receive the honor.

The Diamondbacks' mascot is D. Baxter the Bobcat. Although a Diamondback is a snake, the mascot took its name from the ballpark's old name, Bank One Ballpark (BOB), and from a play on words: D. Bax-ter (D-backs).

GLOSSARY

ace

A team's best starting pitcher.

acquire

To receive a player through trade or by signing as a free agent.

contract

A binding agreement about, for example, years of commitment by a baseball player in exchange for a given salary.

draft

A system used by professional sports leagues to select new players in order to spread incoming talent among all teams.

expansion

In sports, to add a franchise or franchises to a league.

free agent

A player free to sign with any team of his choosing after his contract expires.

postseason

Games played in the playoffs by the top teams after the regular-season schedule has been completed.

promising

Filled with hope and potential.

prospect

A young player, usually one who has little major league experience.

retire

To officially end one's career.

retractable

Can be opened or closed mechanically depending on the weather.

rookie

A first-year professional athlete.

veteran

An individual with great experience in a particular endeavor.

wiry

Thin and small, but strong.

FOR MORE INFORMATION

Further Reading

Euchner, Charles. *The Last Nine Innings: Inside the Real Game Fans Never See.* Chicago: Sourcebooks, 2006.

Johnson, Randy, and Jim Rosenthal. *Randy Johnson's Power Pitching: The Big Unit's Secrets to Domination, Intimidation, and Winning.* New York: Three Rivers Press, 2003.

Travers, Steven, and Andy Dorf. *Diamondbacks Essential: Everything You Need to Know to Be a Real Fan!* Chicago: Triumph Books, 2007.

Web Links

To learn more about the Arizona Diamondbacks, visit ABDO Publishing Company online at **www.abdopublishing.com**. Web sites about the Diamondbacks are featured on our Book Links page. These links are routinely monitored and updated to provide the most current information available.

Places to Visit

Chase Field
401 East Jefferson Street
Phoenix, Arizona 85004
602-462-6700
www.azchasefield.com
This has been the Diamondbacks' home stadium for their entire history. The team plays 81 regular-season home games here each year.

Diamondbacks Spring Training
Salt River Fields at Talking Stick
7555 North Pima Road
Scottsdale, AZ 85256
480-270-5000
www.saltriverfields.com
This new spring-training field was under construction as of 2010 and was scheduled to be ready for spring 2011. The Diamondbacks were to share the facility with the Colorado Rockies.

National Baseball Hall of Fame and Museum
25 Main Street
Cooperstown, NY 13326
1-888-HALL-OF-FAME
www.baseballhall.org
This hall of fame and museum highlights the greatest players and moments in the history of baseball.

INDEX

About the Author

Rob Tricchinelli is a former newspaper copy editor and an aspiring lawyer. He attends Cornell Law School in Ithaca, New York. He previously worked as a copy editor at the *Baltimore Sun* and the *Washington Post*. Tricchinelli has also worked for National Public Radio's legal department and has written freelance news and sports articles in Maryland. This is his first book.